"Joan Kavanaugh is a spirit-filled poet whose masterful use of language conveys a deep wisdom that lights up the worship service in prophetic Riverside Church. Her public prayers inspire us all!"

—CORNEL WEST, Professor of Philosophy and Christian Practice, Union Theological Seminary

"Joan Kavanaugh is that rare clergyperson who touches the personal and global, weaving together poetry, activism, and a profound degree of openness to the human experience. Not only did I love this book for my personal reading, I will turn to it again and again as I lead my congregation in public prayer for God's broken world. Simply stated: every minister should have a copy in his or her library!"

—R. SCOTT COLGLAZIER, Senior Minister, First Congregational Church of Los Angeles

"Joan Kavanaugh's eloquent prayers provide a prophetic and sweeping vision of human possibility in an impossibly conflicted world. They call us to live in the presence of a God whose love is radically inclusive, giving voice to our perennial longing for justice and deep connection."

—SAM KEEN, author of *In the Absence of God* and *Fire in the Belly*

"Combining poetic wit, prophetic passion, and pastoral wisdom, Joan Kavanaugh prays us into spaces of imagination that are rare and wonderful. She shows us what it means to be human; she gives us an anatomy of our souls. And she shows us what it means to live together; she gives us a map of the world. With our souls and world map in hand, she prays us into the arms of God, and lets us see life eternal in the here and now."

—SERENE JONES, President, Union Theological Seminary

For the Living of These Days

For the Living
of These Days

Prayers for a Troubled World

JOAN L. KAVANAUGH

Foreword by James A. Forbes Jr.

CASCADE *Books* · Eugene, Oregon

FOR THE LIVING OF THESE DAYS
Prayers for a Troubled World

Cascade Books
An Imprint of Wipf and Stock Publishers
199 W. 8th Ave., Suite 3
Eugene, OR 97401

www.wipfandstock.com

ISBN 13: 978-1-62032-194-2

Cataloguing-in-Publication data:

Kavanaugh, Joan L.

    For the living of these days : prayers for a troubled world / Joan L. Kavanaugh.

    xvi + 108 pp. ; 23 cm.

    ISBN 13: 978-1-62032-194-2

    1. Pastoral prayers. 2. Riverside Church (New York, NY) I. Forbes, James, 1935–. II. Title.

BV250 K10 2012

Manufactured in the U.S.A.

For
John, companion of my soul,
Lauren, who helped make this book possible,
and all the good people of The Riverside Church

Contents

Contents

Foreword

The Riverside Church is renowned for the consistently high quality of preaching from the pulpit, the exceptionally rich musicality of its organists and choirs, and the prophetic relevance of its social justice ministry. This collection of prayers by Joan L. Kavanaugh reflects another dimension of distinction in worship: the power of public prayer. Strikingly honest and thoughtful, her prayers address a wide range of contemporary issues with prophetic vision, pastoral sensitivity, and theological grounding.

During my tenure as Senior Minister, there was a rotation among the clergy as to who would offer the pastoral prayer each week. They all did their best to carry out this responsibility under the guidance of the Spirit, while bringing their best literary skills to the task. Sometimes parishioners would ask for a copy of the pastoral prayer. Most frequently, it was Dr. Kavanaugh whose prayers were requested. After a while, Joan was urged by many of us to publish her prayers so that others could be inspired by them. Upon her retirement as Director of Riverside's Counseling Center, she was almost mandated to prepare her prayers for publication. This collection of prayers for a troubled world will be treasured well beyond Riverside.

The remarkable thing about these prayers is the way they chronicle signal events impacting the life of the church, the nation, and the global community. Out of her intimate knowledge of congregational concerns, Joan had her finger on the pulse of those who gathered weekly to worship. As a part of the clergy team, she knew the ins and outs of our hopes and dreams, stresses and strains. In the course of time, I began to observe in Joan's ministry of pastoral prayer what seemed like a ministerial charism of intercessory prayer. Romans chapter 8 speaks of our inability to pray as we ought, and we are therefore given the aid of the Spirit in finding the longed-for expression:

> Likewise, the Spirit helps us in our weakness: for we do not know how to pray as we ought, but that very Spirit intercedes with sighs too deep for words. And God who searches the heart knows what is the mind of the Spirit, because the Spirit intercedes for the saints according to the will of God" (Romans 8:26–27).

These prayers are Spirit-inspired. Observe the breadth and depth of concerns, the alertness to current events and themes in our human struggle. Note Joan's faithfulness to the theological foundation of the tradition, her passionate concern for the well-being of parishioners and the larger human community, her openness to hear what the Spirit has to say to us, especially in times of deep suffering and turmoil. When words are inspired by the Spirit, people recognize that the longings of their own hearts have found a voice of truth and grace. And when the people say "Amen," it is more than a formality for ending a prayer; it is an acknowledgement that the Spirit has discerned the longing within and has supplied the words, feelings, and fulfillment of God's promise "for the living of these days."

At its best, prayer generates honesty and self-reflection, courage and hope, deep connection and healing. Prayer empowers us to become better human beings, closer to discovering that God's love is for everyone. Joan Kavanaugh's prayers capture this Spirit.

Dr. James A. Forbes Jr.

Preface

On my retirement from The Riverside Church in New York City, an older African American woman, a member for over fifty years, called me her "prayer warrior." I was moved and humbled, as I was when so many parishioners asked that my prayers be published. In our Riverside tradition, the pastoral prayer in worship is intended to be the people's prayer—gathering up our longings, our fears, our failings, our hopes. It is an invitation to spend a moment in the presence of God's love, and to search out God's intentions for us. In prayer, we dare to ask what God expects of us; to be mindful of what we should aspire to, if there is truly a spark of the divine in every flawed one of us. In this spirit, prayer opens our hearts to what is essential, to what is at the core of our humanity, if we are made in God's image.

This book is a collection of prayers for a troubled world, in Harry Emerson Fosdick's words, "for the living of these days." In writing the prayers, I always begin by asking myself, "What do we need to pray about this day, this week, in the midst of our current human condition and struggle?" The prayers are written "with a Bible in one hand, and a newspaper in the other." I try to be focused and truthful, because in prayer it is God we invite into our hearts. And it is we who must seek to rework ourselves into something a little closer to God's intentions for us. Prayer is our attempt to seek God's light in the darkness of our world, and of our souls. To grope for wisdom and meaning. To find a center, a calm in the storm. To experience God's grace in the midst of brokenness. To express awe and gratitude. To be changed. To reshape our lives, our desires and behaviors in a manner that is more compatible with God's love for all of us: every person, of every color, creed, and culture.

God's intentions for us are quite clear: to love God and love our neighbors, the whole conflicted human community, as ourselves. To do justice, love mercy, walk humbly with a God who belongs to all of us in this post-9/11 world that is so filled with arrogance and religious intolerance. We pray with humility only when we recognize that there are many pathways to God, and all of them need repair.

Abraham Heschel once said, "Prayer may not save us, but prayer makes us worth saving." The prayers in this book try to speak to many of the issues of our times: "evils" that are as eternal as they are specific to our current struggles. These evils are the oldest, most intractable and universal of human failings, global now in scope and difficulty: greed and exploitation, oppression and racism, poverty and violence, injustice and indifference. They call on all of us to look at the abyss within as well as the anguish without. They invite us to call upon God for guidance; to admit how lost we are on our own. They require an "adult" faith in a God who cannot rescue us, or protect us, but who can empower us with the tools of love, and courage, and compassion. A God who is waiting for our healing and redemption, showing us the way. A God of grace and infinite love.

The prayers remind us, in Martin Luther King's words, that "Darkness cannot drive out darkness; only light can do that. And hate cannot drive out hate; only love can do that." My prayers borrow words and insights from many teachers and prophets, biblical and modern, among them William Sloane Coffin and James A. Forbes. Both of these spiritual leaders shaped the clay of my soul during their years at

Riverside. I am grateful for their prophetic brilliance, and for the love they brought into so many lives, my own included. Most of all, I am grateful to the Riverside congregation for its consistent, if arduous, journey towards trying to become a beloved community, where barriers are gradually dismantled, and every person is valued as a child of God.

These prayers are for everyone who joins in that worthy struggle.

Joan L. Kavanaugh
June 2012

The phrase "For the Living of These Days" and the quotations in the chapter headings are all borrowed from the hymn "God of Grace and God of Glory," authored by the first Senior Minister of The Riverside Church, Dr. Harry Emerson Fosdick.

420 God of Grace and God of Glory

CWM RHONDDA   8.7.8.7.8.7.7

Harry Emerson Fosdick, 1930; alt.   John Hughes, 1907

1. God of grace and God of glo - ry, On Thy peo - ple
2. Lo! the hosts of e - vil round us Scorn Thy Christ, as -
3. Cure Thy chil - dren's war - ring mad - ness, Bend our pride to
4. Set our feet on loft - y pla - ces; Gird our lives that

pour Thy power; Crown Thine an - cient chur - ch's sto - ry;
sail Thy ways! From the fears that long have bound us
Thy con - trol; Shame our wan - ton, self - ish glad - ness,
they may be Ar - mored with all Christ - like gra - ces,

Bring its bud to glo - rious flower. Grant us wis - dom, grant us cour - age,
Free our hearts to faith and praise. Grant us wis - dom, grant us cour - age,
Rich in things and poor in soul. Grant us wis - dom, grant us cour - age,
Pledged to set all cap - tives free. Grant us wis - dom, grant us cour - age,

For the fac - ing of this hour, For the fac - ing of this hour.
For the liv - ing of these days, For the liv - ing of these days.
Lest we miss Thy king-dom's goal, Lest we miss Thy king-dom's goal.
That we fail not them nor Thee! That we fail not them nor Thee!

One

The World in Crisis
"Grant Us Wisdom, Grant Us Courage"

*All meaningful and lasting change
begins on the inside.*

—Martin Luther King Jr.

9/11

E ternal God: Shepherd, Redeemer, Savior,
This morning we need You, and we need each other.
Let us join in a moment of silence and solidarity with all
who have died and all who love them, for our hearts are
with them.

O God of life . . .
Today we return to You from a wasteland of terror and
     violence and cruelty.
We come as refugees . . . lost and stunned.
We come thirsty and hungry for You.
We come with fear for our future and for our children.
We come feeling vulnerable, our safety shattered along
     with our towers of economic and military strength.
We come from a world torn apart by rising fanaticism,
     intolerance, and injustice.
We come in frustration and anger, and a deep, deep
     sadness.

And yet, even through the unspeakable horror of this
     week, You have clearly been with us.
We have seen *Your* presence in the heroism and courage of
     rescuers who risked their own lives for strangers.
We have seen *Your* face in the exhausted faces of firemen
     and policemen and rescue workers who toiled be-
     yond exhaustion to find survivors.

We have seen *Your* love in the rivers of generosity and
compassion that poured through thousands of volun-
teers who went to help with gifts of medical aid and
blood, food, socks, and prayers.

We have seen *Your* courage in the brave passengers who
sacrificed their own lives to save countless others.

We have seen with our own eyes this week that You are
with us in the valley of the shadow of death, in the
presence of our enemies.

We have seen You in the power of our deepened sense of
connection with each other, transcending all that we
ever, in pettier moments, allowed to divide us.

It has been a dark week, winds of evil blowing that we
have smelled in the very air around us. And now we turn
to You to be that light, that inextinguishable light that will
overcome this darkness of ours. In these desperate times,
when the world is endangered and hope seems small, and
the tides of revenge are running high, we need Your light
and wisdom to show us the way forward.

You are not the God of hate we have seen worshiped this
week. You are the God of life. And as our nation strategizes
its response, we must all remember that You place before
us life and death, and You ask us always to choose life.

Teach us, and our world community, what this means.
Teach us before it is too late that violence begets violence,
and that these new forms of warfare have no victors.
Teach us that we are perpetrators of violence as well as
its victims, that we cannot isolate ourselves from
suffering in this world or live in relative luxury for
ourselves alone.

Teach us that fanatics and terrorists are born under conditions of suffering and injustice and poverty.

Teach us that religious fanaticism of all persuasions always
has, and always will have, a high body count.

Teach us that hatred ceases not when it is met with hatred,
but when it is met with justice and compassion.

If we really want to root out terrorists, we must go not
merely to their cells and training camps but to the
conditions of human injustice and dogmatic arrogance that breed terrorism in the first place.

Teach us to be wary of turning our enemies into Satan, lest
we find that we are infected with the same cancer.

Teach us to demonize no country or religion; for God, You
speak to all of us, not in English or Arabic or Hebrew,
but in the universal language of human suffering.

Teach our world leaders to listen to the voices of suffering
if they want to build a coalition for a peaceful and
secure world.

Teach us to be moderate and wise.

Teach us that love is our most essential, perhaps our only,
means of survival.

O God of love and life, Thy Kingdom come, Thy will be
done.

Give us sufficient light to see Your will.

Reenter our lives that we might put goodness, not ven-
geance, at the center.

Center our lives on faith, not fear.

When our strength wanes, help us to rely upon Yours.

For in the power of Your love, we are afflicted but not
crushed, persecuted but not forsaken, struck down
but not destroyed. Your love will heal our broken
places and make us whole again.

We pray for the healing of the whole world, including our
    enemies.
Make us all instruments of a lasting peace.
Amen.

Facing Terrorism

God of Healing and Redemption,

We come today seeking guidance and strength. A storm has broken in our country and in the world, challenging our most basic assumptions. And we have not yet seen the full strength of this storm. Our country is shaken. Our easy optimism is shaken. Our prosperity and economic strength are shaken. Our religious institutions are shaken. An angry, vengeful David whom we cannot even see—a David armed with a slingshot full of unknown horrors—is aiming right at our Goliath. We are dismayed at the ease with which a rogue band of fanatical terrorists is disrupting the world we call "civilized."

O God, we come before You today with many questions, afraid of the unknown. Our military is bombing a hidden enemy whose strength and appeal is surely fueled by injustice and poverty and ignorance. Our world is small. Has it awakened a sleeping giant of hatred brewed in a clash between ancient cultures and modern ways? Will it ever be possible for people of different faiths and cultures to see that we worship one God? Will we ever understand that You, the living God, ask us to look into each other's eyes— Jewish, Christian, Muslim eyes, eyes of any faith—and see in those eyes our brothers and our sisters? Can we claim to believe in You who loves each and every one of us, and yet live in a world that tolerates such a discrepancy between rich and poor, privilege and suffering?

Do we dare, all who call ourselves religious, to be a peaceful people of God, fighting fanaticism and terror and suffering with the weapons of faith and tolerance and compassion? Can our Goliath nation that consumes more than its share of the world's supplies look at itself as part of the problem, understanding our own role in the evil that has been unleashed? Can we build a coalition of nations that will outlaw terrorism and violence, yet listen to the voices of suffering to build a new vision: a new kind of Kingdom?

O God, You are an inextinguishable light in this fractured world. And Yours is the only Kingdom we can trust. You are the God who loves us all, and we cannot follow Your will if we are filled with hatred. For if we hate, then we cannot follow what You have asked us to do: serve justice, love mercy, and walk humbly with our God. We cannot be arrogant and walk humbly with You.

We pray today for all who are caught in this madness—for men and women in the military, for the leaders who must build a common vision, for the many innocent people being killed in Afghanistan and other parts of our world. We pray for the terrorists and for the misguided clerics who incite them. Deliver us all, O God, from danger. May Your divine love enter all our hearts and transform our precious world. Help us to be a loving community for each other in these vulnerable times. Thy Kingdom come. Thy will be done.

We ask this in the name of Jesus.
Amen.

A Thanksgiving for New York City

God of Redemption,

We come from the North and South, East and West, but we gather together today as New Yorkers. Once again our city is grieving. Smoke still rises from Ground Zero. The bagpipes continue to mourn our firefighters, and we will not soon stop grieving lives lost by the thousands, and lives affected by the scores of thousands.

But amidst all this grief, O God, we feel Your presence and Your love, healing us, holding us all together. For grief has welded us into one family, one body of humanity, and this season of grief is also a season of thanksgiving for all that we have and for all that we are. In this wonderful city of ours, whose body has been attacked, the soul grows ever stronger.

In the soul of our city,

> We rely on You, the living God, in a multitude of prayers and songs and rituals. We worship You in the fasts of Ramadan and the feasts of Thanksgiving, in the intimate temples of Hindu gods and Buddhist meditations, in the churches and synagogues and mosques, in the richness of different languages and accents, and in the diversity of many traditions. And we see that You are the God who belongs to all of us and loves all of us. Thank You for this gift.

In the soul of our city,

> We welcome a future which relies on our strengths:
> our tolerance, our faith communities, our racial and
> ethnic diversity, the deep kindness and courage that
> graces us and comes to us from people of many eth-
> nicities, from voices of many accents.

In the soul of our city,

> We see that our deepest strength is not material, but
> collective. And what is indispensable to our city is
> the development of our capacity to see Your divine
> creation at work in people of every color and creed.
> Thank You for this gift.

In the soul of our city,

> We know that rebuilding cannot rely solely on the
> recovery of prosperity. It must rely on the good
> will of men and women who will ensure that the
> poor are the first, not the last, to benefit. It must
> rely on a vision of justice big enough to include us
> all—privileged and poor—in a safety net of human
> compassion and connections. For we now see clearly
> from far away Afghanistan that whatever affects
> one of us affects all of us. We have seen the power
> of hatred reach across the world and destroy towers
> and lives. Now we must trust in the power of love to
> reach across the world to reshape rubble into a world
> of decency and hope. As the burkas are lifted, we see
> that the smiling faces of Afghani women are the faces
> of our sisters. We see that when the children of Af-
> ghanistan and Iraq are fed, our children will be safer.
> This world is now so small; perhaps our vision will
> improve: united we stand; divided we fall. And so,
> O God, for all the small signs of hope this week—

for aid workers rescued, for new alliances with former enemies, for nuclear stockpiles reduced, for fresh glimpses of the truth that we are all in this together and must learn to live together, we give You thanks.

O God of compassion and love, help us to remember that nothing separates us from Your love. Guide us as we struggle to create a new world that better reflects Your love and Your justice.
Amen.

Called to Life

G od of Hope, God of Life,

Come to us this morning as we worship together. Come as vision. Come as hope. Come as resurrection. Call us to new life.

We come from many weeks of escalating violence in the Middle East. From increasing religious violence and intolerance in many parts of the world. From the threat of a whole new generation of nuclear weapons, poised for use.

O God of life, sometimes our world seems so committed to death! And so today we come to You, hungry for Your healing spirit. Hungry for guidance. Hungry for hope. Hungry for transformation.

When You created us, O God, You breathed life into us. Help us to claim this sacred gift of life as something that belongs to every living being on this earth. Help us to see that when You breathed life into us, You intended to make every living person a sacred vessel. In creating us to be human, made in Your image, You gave us dominion over the fish and plants and animals, but not over each other. Help us to see that our richly varied faiths and cultures and colors are *all* sacred to You. Teach us that if we are all sacred, then we surely have no right to the death penalty or to the imposition of power and dominance through nuclear,

biological, and chemical weapons of mass destruction.
If we are all sacred, then how can we justify dominance:
Islamist over "infidel," Israeli over Palestinian, American
over developing world, free over slave, white over people
of color, men over women, or any religion over another's
pathway to faith?

O God of resurrection, call us, like Lazarus, back to life!

Call us to respect.
Call us to understanding and compassion.
Call us to a more inclusive justice.
Call us to generosity.
Call us to develop strategic aid, rather than strategic
    nuclear weapons.
Call us to a world where every living person must be
    fed and clothed, housed and educated, and
    treated with dignity.
Call us to develop leadership and vision.
Call us to create a world in which we nurture
    the deep human connections that transcend our
    differences.
Call us to forgiveness.
Call us to embrace a peace that can sustain this earth
    for all of us.

We pray today for all the innocent victims of terrorism
and war. We pray for those serving in the military. We pray
for our immigrants. We pray for all who are grieving. And
this week we pray especially for world leaders to find the
courage and the vision to choose peace and to choose life.

O loving God, our faith in You sustains us. Embrace us all
with hope and with courage.

In Jesus' name we pray.
Amen.

Keeping the Faith

God of Mercy, God of Love, God of Peace,

This morning we gather as a community of faith, and we need to be in prayer.

Help us, O God, to keep the faith.

> In our tumultuous world, once again on the verge of war, the pain of the world lies heavy upon us. The future brings terrible uncertainty for all of us and for all our children—the children of America and Iraq, Palestine and Israel—for the children of all the nations. Our own nation—the most powerful on earth—is both recalcitrant and vulnerable. Open debate has become "unpatriotic." The loud drums of war drown out the voices of conscience. Leaders are afraid to speak their minds and listen to their hearts. We would rather attack the "evil empire" *out there* than face the common evil *within* shared by all of us: the chasm between rich and poor; the degradation of the environment; a world awash in weapons of mass destruction; the self-serving, tribal thinking that deceives us into believing that we are not all brothers and sisters and neighbors with the same human needs.

Help us, O God, to keep the faith.

To become people who are *willing* to be faithful to You. For faith is a decision. You have tried so hard to show us what You require of the faithful. Jesus taught us to love You and to love each other. To reach out to our neighbors. To be Samaritans, willing to help the wounded and victimized along the roads and pathways of our own lives. You are so clear, O God. And we are so stubborn! Our complicity in sin is so huge! O God, can You really forgive us? Is Your forgiveness and love for us that generous?

Help us, O God, to keep the faith.
> Lead us through this wilderness we have made. Transform us, if we are willing, with Your love. Help us to be guided by Your love of all peoples and races and nations. Help all of us, so divided by faith and tribe, inequality and ancient hatreds, to become tolerant and inclusive. Teach us to renounce violence of all kinds, not just the violence of war and the evil of terrorism, but the abuses of power and privilege.

Help us, O God, to keep the faith.
> Here in our own church community. To be better friends to each other. To be forgiving and tolerant. To see each other, in all our differences and imperfections, as loved by You. To eat and drink from Your abundance and to *live* from Your abundance, so that we can share generously with each other. Help us as church members, old and new, to forge a community of faith that leaves no one out. Infuse us with Your love and acceptance.

Help all of us, O God, to keep the faith.
Amen.

In the Advent of War

God of Blessings,

Long ago, you came to us in the blessing of a child of brilliant promise, born into a world filled, then as now, with terrorism and danger. He came as Savior and as Hope.

In this season of Advent, we find ourselves anxiously waiting.

> Waiting in the darkness of fear.
> Waiting for inspectors to find weapons of mass
>   destruction.
> Waiting for a war that fills the world with dread.
> Waiting for the next terrorist attack.
> Waiting for the economy to turn around.
> Waiting for the next disaster to strike.

But as we gather this morning in Your church, in the cradle of our faith, we believe that You are here with us. And we await the miracle of the Christ child, born to save us from ourselves. In this season of vulnerability and hope, help us to find the wisdom to make that ancient, eternal journey to seek the powerful light of a child born into a suffering world. A child born to bring peace.

Come to us now, O God, as war once again threatens our world. Help all of us to choose life over death. Help us to understand that we are deeply, globally intertwined in a struggle of identities. And killing each other, killing each other's children, is no way to survive. We need to choose life!

O God, call us out of darkness into Your great light. We are all broken. Help us to allow our brokenness to let in Your light. Help us to be guided by that child, born into poverty, sent to teach us how to become more human. He believed in us. Help us to believe in ourselves.

> Jesus came as fellow sufferer and as healer. Helping the blind to see, the paralyzed to walk, the wounded to be more whole.
> He came to teach us compassion and mutual respect.
> He came to show us how to be forgiving and inclusive and generous.
> He came to lead us out of the wilderness of war and brutality and oppression.
> He came to free the prisoners, to challenge poverty and injustice.
> He came to teach us to love each other, to treat each other as we would be treated.
> He came to bless the peacemakers and the meek and the pure in heart. He would be appalled by the concentration of so much wealth in the hands of so few.
> He came to challenge evil and dogma, to remind us that we are all connected.
> He came to show all faiths that there are many doorways to God but only one God: the God who loves all of us!

Help us, O God, to learn. You brought us the light. Help us to keep the light kindled in the darkness. We give thanks for the blessing of Your unfailing presence in our lives. Amen.

At War with Iraq

A Prayer for Peace

Eternal God,

You are Mother and Father of us all: every person, every race, every nation, every faith. When will we ever learn? As we join in worship this morning, we are once again at war.

> Capable of turning swords into plowshares, we worship the sword.
> Capable of insight and restraint, we are blinded by arrogance and grandiosity.
> Capable of negotiation, we are addicted to power.

In these perilous times, we turn to You for wisdom, for courage, for vision, perhaps even for a miracle. Long ago, You sent Your Son to remind us that despite all the evidence of our failures, our sinfulness, You had not abandoned us. Come to us now, as danger looms large. Help the leaders of our country and our world to relinquish the tactics of aggression and war. Help our leaders to temper power with responsibility, to act with clear knowledge that each action we take affects the whole world and its future.

You have commanded: Thou shall not kill.

> Teach us that we divided human beings must learn to
> live in peace. That war breeds endless cycles of
> mistrust and violence.
>
> Teach us to be so stricken by the human cost of war
> that we might abhor its use.
>
> Teach us that when we go to battle for pride or profit,
> all we really win is enemies.
>
> Teach us that prosperity built on the suffering of oth-
> ers is ultimately doomed. That what we reap is
> resentment and revenge.
>
> Teach us to fight with great courage for peace and for
> human dignity.
>
> Teach us to understand those prophetic words:
> hatred ceases only when it is met with love and
> justice.
>
> Teach us to restrain our anger and thereby harness a
> power that can change the world.
>
> Teach us to battle not among the nations but within
> our own minds and hearts. For when we wage
> battle against selfishness or greed or injustice,
> then even the smallest triumph benefits the
> whole world.

Today we pray for the courage to address oppression and
injustice. For victory over terrorism will be won only when
the world is a better place for all its displaced and dispos-
sessed citizens.

Teach us, O God, that we are *all* Your children and that
violence is never Your way. We pray today for all the victims of this tragic war. For all the brave soldiers, American
and Iraqi, for all the innocent men and women who must

fight this war and bear its terrible consequences. Families weep tonight in the United States, in Iraq, and in many other countries of the world. We pray for the grieving, for the children, for the orphans and widows, for the displaced and the maimed, for all who have died and will die.

O God, help us to become one whole and human family. Help us to preserve this world for its future generations.

In the words of Saint Francis,

> Lord, make us instruments of Thy peace.
> Where there is hatred, let us sow love;
> Where there is injury, pardon;
> Where there is doubt, faith;
> Where there is despair, hope;
> Where there is darkness, light;
> Where there is sadness, joy.

Lord, make us instruments of Thy peace.
In Christ's name we pray.
Amen.

Invocation

United in Sin[1]

O God,

We come to You this morning for refuge and for strength. We gather from a world where nations are raging and mighty kingdoms are unraveling. It has been a week of shocking abuse and humiliation and brutality. A week that saddens and shames us with the painful evidence that we are united in sin with the very enemies we seek to demonize!

O God, teach us all to be humble enough to listen for that still, small voice in our hearts that is Your voice. Open our ears and eyes to the suffering we inflict on others through our arrogance and fear. Remove our blindness to our own culpability in a world that has veered so dangerously off course.

Bless us with courage to address and disarm the hatreds and injustices that so endanger this precious world that belongs to all of us. Grant us wisdom and courage for the living of these days.
Amen.

---

1. Offered in the aftermath of the exposé of American brutality at the Abu Ghraib Prison.

Cain and Abel

Faithful and Loving God,

We come this morning seeking Your wisdom, Your presence. Enter our hearts today, for it is in the heart that You speak to all who will listen.

> You speak with a love that is always with us.
> You speak through the human soul that is always attacked, but not destroyed.
> You speak through truth.
> You speak through the quiet courage that guides us through our worst times.
> You cry out to be heard in this insanity of escalating violence: nation against nation, faith against faith, sect against sect, brother against brother, sister against sister.
> You speak in the voice of hope and the assurance of unfailing love.
> You speak in the transforming power of the human soul.

Today, You speak to us in the story of Cain and Abel. Help us to listen. Help us to learn that the line dividing good and evil runs through each of our hearts. Help us to see that each of us is oppressed and oppressor. Teach us that no one wins at another's expense. Help us to learn that greed is violent, and poverty is violent, and dehumanization is violent. Help us to see that the blood of abuse is flowing in our land with our guns and our nuclear weapons and our arrogance. And You are crying out to us, "What have you done?!"

O God, help us not to be deceived and blinded by propaganda. Teach us that our survival and strength depend not on military might or nuclear weapons, but on wisdom and inclusivity, justice and generosity. Teach all the warring faiths and factions of our world to seek common ground.

Today we pray for new insights, new pathways, new eyes to see the insanity of our violent, warring ways. We pray for the strength to build a different kind of world, and for the wisdom to begin with ourselves. We pray for peace. We pray for leaders in the United States, in Iraq and Iran, in Israel and Palestine, in North Korea and China, and all over the world who will dare to be voices for moderation and reconciliation and hope. We pray for all, especially in Iraq, who must suffer the devastating consequences of war and escalating violence. May Your wisdom guide us, Your forgiveness humble us, Your love empower us to change. Amen.

Hurricane Katrina

God of Hope, God of Love,

Today we come home to You, gathering once again in this challenging and challenged community of faith.

> We come because we need You. Because You sustain us with Your unfailing love, day after day, season after season.
>
> We come from a devastating hurricane season where we have witnessed the terrible unfolding of a national tragedy—from catastrophic flooding to the catastrophic failure of our country to treat its own citizens, black and white, rich and poor, as one nation under God.
>
> We come from a land of division, in which prejudice prevails, privilege wields power, and the poor and powerless are abandoned in crisis, as they are in all the other seasons of their lives.
>
> We come from the stark reality of failed levees,
>> failed responsibility,
>> failed promises,
>> failed compassion that left the poor, the critically ill, and the powerless old to die on their own.
>
> We come from a system of response as broken as those levees, where the mostly white people of

privilege do just fine, and the mostly black poor
are left behind.

We come from the reality that "what went wrong"
was our tragic failure to pay attention as a nation to Your most fundamental requirement:
"Above all things, have unfailing love towards
one another."

And so, O God, we come home today to find our
strength in Your strength.

We all come as refugees and as sinners needing
Your acceptance and forgiveness. Needing the
transforming pull of Your love to keep us from a
flood of despair.

We come to petition Your help in transforming this
country of broken promises; this world of elu-
sive justice and warring ideologies and faiths.

We come to be reminded that You call us to a Kingdom where the first shall be the last, and the last
first. That You call us to solidarity with all who
suffer from oppression and neglect.

We come to be empowered by the essential truth that
we are *all* worth saving. That You call us to be
neighbors to each other in suffering.

We come because You remind us of what our arrogance denies: that the whole human community
deserves our compassion and our respect. That
military might will never win where morality
has failed. That the poor and the powerless are
a diaspora, which the nations of privilege must
gather in to move towards justice and inclusivity
and hope. This is the true nature of the transformation You ask of our nation and our world.

And so today, O God, we ask for Your blessing and for Your help. Help us to be guided by a spirit of generosity and truth as we pledge our support and resources to a world in desperate need of peace and reconciliation. Help us to be peacemakers here, in our own congregation, as well as in the nation, and in the larger world. We pray for the courage to lead and for the humility to follow.

O God, we know that when we pass through the raging waters, we will not be overwhelmed. And when we pass through the fires, we shall not be consumed, for You have promised to be with us. May we all come to feel the transforming power of this enduring love.
Amen.

A Prayer for Guidance

God of Peace and Love,

We come to worship today because You gather us all in with acceptance and compassion. You are the God who will not rebuke us: who nurtures our starving souls with Your steadfast love. Who sees all of our faces—young and old, black and white, gay and straight, privileged and poor—as the faces of people all made in Your divine image.

We come to be forgiven. To be reassured once again that we are all worth saving despite deep flaws and failures. We come because You carry us through times of darkness with arms of sustaining love. Because Your light provides the vision that can set free the mercy and compassion that lie dormant in all of us. We come because our lives are empty without You. We come because we are grateful!

We also come for Your guidance. Long ago, You sent Moses to lead the people of God out of slavery and oppression to a land of promise and hope. Today our land of promise and hope is threatened. And we have no Moses! We are thwarted by leaders of little faith and vision. We are threatened by the abuse and corruption of concentrated power.

By illegal wars of aggression.
By the undermining of basic civil rights and liberties.

By the abandonment of protections for the powerless.
By a health system that leaves millions out.
By a child protection system that allowed seven-
year-old Nixzmary to be beaten to death over a
missing yogurt.
By an education system that fails many of our
children.
By a divided nation still enslaved by injustice and
greed and discrimination.

And so today, O God, we turn to You. Teach us to become disciples of the Jesus who taught us that we are all brothers and sisters. Who taught us to love. Who came "to bring good news to the poor, to proclaim release to the captives, the recovery of sight to the blind; to set at liberty those who are oppressed, to proclaim the acceptable Year of the Lord."

Help us, in our deeply polarized nation and world, to embody Your divine love, through which the repair of the world is possible and the devastation of generations can be healed. Today we pray for peace among nations and tribes, factions and faiths. We pray for all who live in the devastating pathways of war and violent conflicts. We pray for this world of ours: for wisdom in our leaders and in the highest court of our land. We pray for Haiti. We pray for peace and health in the African continent, especially in Sudan. We pray for all who are still suffering from the devastations of natural disasters. We pray that we might become better stewards of this world You have entrusted to our care.
Amen.

Presidential Election

God of Hope,
We pray for new beginnings.
Watch over us today. Watch over us this week! Watch over this turning point in our church, in our nation, in our world. There is so much at stake!

> Guide our feet, Lord, while we run this race,
> 'cause we don't wanna run this race in vain.[2]

O God, this world of ours has lost its way.

> Threatened by financial meltdown.
> Fractured by reckless greed.
> At war for increasingly scarce resources.
> Torn asunder by religious and ideological
> intolerance.

We pray today for new leadership.

> For vision.
> For transformation.
> For our divided nation to come together and find
> new strength, new voices, new ideas and priori-
> ties. New trust and cooperation. New energy
> and hope.

---

2. From the African American Spiritual "Guide My Feet."

In this critical election, may the better angels of our nature prevail. May we in this nation finally realize the dream of judging by content of character, not color of skin. May hope triumph over fear. Restraint and wisdom over arrogance. May we all be guided by Your most fundamental law—to love You and love our neighbors as ourselves. May we find the courage and the wisdom to elect a president who will bring unity to our nation, generosity and healing to our battered world.

> Guide our feet, Lord, while we run this race,
> 'cause we don't wanna run this race in vain.

Teach us and our elected leaders how to follow this path. How to leave behind the pathway of indifference and isolation, and replace it with compassion and connection. On your path, O God, You ask us to overcome division and class warfare. You ask us to confront all the ways in which we benefit from privilege and exploitation. You ask us to honor the least among us. You ask us to be humble and just. You ask us to understand just how interdependent we all are.

And so today, O God, we pray for guidance and for faith that this is not an impossible dream. The obstacles are powerful. They live within each one of us, fueled by arrogance and fear, by entrenched power, by apathy, by ignorance, by the poverty of our imagination, and the smallness of our dreams.

As our nation prepares to face its next challenges, especially in our own backyard, help us, O God, to embrace the simple truths that show us the way. Show us how to have big enough dreams. Show us what it means to *act* as if we are all created in Your image. Show us what this would mean to our criminal justice system, to our schools, to employment and health care.

Help us, in this coming week, to elect a president who will contribute to the healing of our fractured nation and the restoration of the vision on which it was founded.

> Guide our feet Lord, while we run this race,
> 'cause we don't wanna run this race in vain.

Amen.

Arab Spring

O God, our Refuge and our Strength,

The times, they are a-changin'.[3] Watch over our tumultuous world in these weeks filled with revolutionary hope and sacrifice and danger. Help us to see, O God, that the world cannot stay the way it is; that we must not stay the way we are.

As we witness the courageous crowds in Libya and Egypt, in Tunisia and Bahrain, in Jordan and Yemen, with others waiting to join the throngs, we see a vast tide of irrepressible human longing—breaking down the dams of oppressive and ruthless regimes. As we listen to the voices of the afflicted and the forgotten, we hear Your voice, O God, speaking through the human hunger for freedom and justice and hope. We see Your Spirit in the daring courage required to topple the Pharaohs of bondage and corruption. You are the God who sees pain and brutality and oppression, and reaches with outstretched hands into the hearts of Your people.

O God, help us, in these times, to confront our own institutional Pharaohs—our own unrestrained oppressors—our own widening gap between the indulgences of the super wealthy and the abandoned needs of the middle class and the poor. Guide us, Lord, lest we lose our way,

---

3. From Bob Dylan's 1964 song "The Times They Are a-Changin'."

and become a nation ruled by the rich for the rich. Help us to find the courage and the moral resources to rebuild our nation into a place of hope for all its citizens, wealthy and poor! Help us to reclaim a vision of justice that includes all of us. Help us to ensure that no one is excluded from housing or health care, education or opportunity. Help us to understand that if we tolerate inequality and poverty and racism, we will always have violence in our midst. For discrimination is violent; exploitation is violent; homelessness is violent; unemployment is violent; hunger is violent, and hopelessness is violent.

These are the forms of violence that harm all of us and can turn the American dream into the American lie. In these challenging times, O God, show us the way! Give us the courage to turn our nation and Your world into a place of hope for every child, every person, every human being created in Your divine image.

Help us all to ride through the storms of these times, centered and grounded in Your love for all of us. Help us to remain calm, as if we are at the hub of a wheel that is gradually turning in the right direction. Help us to remember that suffering is not an individual matter . . . it requires all of us to pull together, guided and strengthened by Your love.

Grant us wisdom and courage and hope for the living of these days.
Amen.

A Prayer for the Holy Land[4]

God of all Tribes and Faiths,

We pray today for a land that has lost its way, cut off from its most human and holy roots. We pray for this contested "promised land" to become a land of promise for all of its people. A land of milk and honey. A land of abundance and opportunity.

Let us not be limited by the failure of imagination as we seek just solutions to entrenched conflicts. Help us to go deeper—to be guided by Your universal love for all Your creation, all of Your children. Help us *all* to seek atonement, at-one-ment. To finally comprehend that we *are* all one. Born not as Israelis or Palestinians, not as Jews, Muslims, Christians, but as babies. As children of one God, one land, where there will never be holy ground until there is common ground.

Help us to understand that You are the God of all, and You will not be mocked: we human beings will always reap what we sow. Help us, O God, to become conscious of what You intend for us, if we are truly made in Your image.

> You do not kill.
> You do not separate.

---

4. Written after a recent journey to Israel/Palestine, to meet with human rights activists on all sides.

You do not build walls.
You do not dehumanize.
You do not terrorize.
You do not bomb buses, or children.
You do not oppress or occupy.
You do not restrict access to shared water and land.
You do not favor one people over another.
You do not sanction violence.
You do not imprison.
You do not bulldoze homes and olive trees.
You do not hate or retaliate.

You are the God who asks one fundamental thing: that we learn to love You by loving each other. You are the God who calls us to become our brother's keeper and our sister's keeper because we *are* our brother, our sister. Help us to see each other rightly, with our hearts, to nurture the compassion and sense of justice that lie dormant within our souls. Help us to move beyond division and dogma. To make room for each other in Your beloved land, sacred to so many. To understand, finally, that it is only through *Your* love that we will ever create a land with a heart big enough for all, where justice will roll down like water. Only then will there be a land of transformation and hope. A land that is holy. God of peace, help us to find peace. Amen.

9/11 Tenth Anniversary

God of all the Nations and all the Faiths,

Today we gather as one human family—of many faiths, many backgrounds and cultures—to renew our faith in Your abiding presence. We come with a common longing in our hearts: that Your love might sustain and transform us, in this world where we do so little to sustain and love each other.

Today we remember that devastating attack that shattered our illusions of invulnerability. Nine-eleven shocked us! Challenged us! Hijacked us into a world of terrorism and fear, anxiety and aggression. Led us to invade Iraq and Afghanistan. To sanction torture. To detain without trial. To demonize Muslims and Arabs. To fear the stranger in our midst. To project evil onto "the other." To deny that we are all perpetrators as well as victims of violence in this world.

O God, we confess that we have lost our way. We have been worshiping golden calves—the false gods of military power and economic strength. We have forgotten that violence will always breed violence. We have abandoned vision and dialogue to fanaticism and polarization. We have allowed the erosion of compassion, the loss of vital connection to each other. We have betrayed our common human needs for opportunity and safety and dignity. We have failed to be a people of faith.

And so today, O God, we come before You humbled. Fear-
ful. Needing You to sweep us into Your loving embrace
and show us the way home to You. Help us to remember
that You created us all with a spark of Your divine Spirit to
guide and shape us. Help us to understand that Your love
is universal and limitless. Help us to look into each other's
faces and see beyond Muslim, Christian, Buddhist, Jew,
Stranger. Help us to see brother, sister. Help us to see Your
face in all the diversity of what You created us to be. Help
us to ignite that spark of divine light that lives deep within
each one of us, that we might find new pathways through
the darkness of these times.

Today, as we pray for peace and transformation in our
world, help us to become the miracles we long for.

To relinquish violence and war.
To let go of hostility and revenge.
To remove the blinders of ideology and dogma.
To rekindle compassion and connection.
To confront the unconscionable poverty and injustice
that will always breed violence in our midst.
To refashion this earth that it might better serve the
needs of every man, every woman, and every
child in it.

We give thanks today for all who listen to the voices of
suffering. For all who make sacrifices to save or improve
the lives of their fellow human beings in this shared world.
For all who would be peacemakers. They bless us with
their courage. As we mourn the thousands who lost their
lives on 9/11, the tens, possibly hundreds, of thousands
who died in the wars that followed, let us acknowledge

that fanaticism is inherently violent. And when we look at the history of our religions, let us remember that there is blood on all our hands. We need now to join our hands together. Teach us, O God, that love for You and for each other is the only thing that will ever make us safe. The human soul is always attacked, but never destroyed, because we are capable of love. Capable of choosing to love.

We pray today for all who lost loved ones in the 9/11 attack and its tragic aftermath of war. We pray for our military and the terrible burden they have carried. We pray for all the peoples of the world—for the many who continue to suffer in pathways of natural disaster; who starve to death in slow, painful famine; who continue to suffer through brutal wars, violent revolutions, and terrible poverty.

O God, we have been pulled apart by sin. Let us join together in love and compassion.
Amen.

Two

In Search of the Beloved Community

"From the Fears That Long Have Bound Us"

Every single one of us is said to be of infinite worth . . .
Each single one of us is a God carrier,
Each one of us God's viceroy.
Can you imagine if we really believed that?
—ARCHBISHOP DESMOND TUTU

Invocation: Bless Us

O God, from our troubled world we gather, hungry for Your presence, Your guidance, Your love.

Bless us with Your divine spirit.

> Open us to the source that empowers us from deep within.
> For deep within all of us lies unimaginable goodness and humility, and the knowledge that we are all Your children, all precious to You.

Bless us with greater knowledge of who You intend us to be.

Bless us with courage to become more connected to You and to each other.

Bless us with insight that we might see each other rightly with our hearts.

Bless us with wisdom that we might move in the direction of our highest potential.

Bless us with peace that we might turn our intelligence toward preserving and sharing the resources of our world.

Bless us with faith that You are with us and within us.

Bless us with the deep transformation that this faith requires of us all.

Amen.

This Little Light of Mine[1]

God of Light and Hope,

Today we gather to give thanks, once again, for Your un-wavering presence in our lives. You are the keeper of our hearts. The one who does not slumber or sleep. The one who watches over us as we come and as we go. The one whose help is there to sustain us, whose light is there to guide us when we walk through the shadows of darkness.

In this season of vulnerability—war, joblessness, homeless-ness, anxiety—, help us to find that light You have placed deep within us, to awaken every human heart. It is there, like a jewel, unblemished, even after being buried deep within the earth for centuries. Even our sinfulness, our selfishness, our brokenness cannot destroy or extinguish this light.

It is a light, the song reminds us, that we must bring out into the world.

> "This little light of mine, I'm gonna let it shine."
> Right here in this church, we're gonna let it shine.
> All around the world, we're gonna let it shine.
> Deep within our hearts, we're gonna let it shine.
> Let it shine; let it shine; let it shine!

---

1. From the Gospel children's song by Harry Dixon Loes (1895–1965) called "This Little Light of Mine."

Help us, O God, to be guided by this light. To see that in our precious time on earth, You surely intend for us to learn how to love each other. To do right by each other. To acknowledge Your light in each other—Christians, Jews, Muslims, Hindus, Buddhists, Atheists, Humanists, all creeds and colors. Help us to use this light to dispel the shadows of prejudice, ignorance, and fear that darken our world. Help us to overcome the dark narratives that project fear and evil onto others by demonizing people of different beliefs and faiths. Help us to see the divine light You have placed in every human heart that we might all be illumined by Your vision of a beloved community, which includes all of us as people of worth.

Today we pray for peace within and peace without. May we use the gifts we have received, and pass on the love that has been given to us. We pray for all the world's leaders. May Your wisdom guide us, Your forgiveness humble us, Your love empower us to change.
Amen.

A Prayer for Our Children

O God, we thank You for gathering us together once again.
You bring water and life to our thirsty souls.
You are our ever present help in times of danger.
And when we feel most afraid or unworthy, there You
are loving us more than we dare imagine, with Your
generous and forgiving heart.

Today, on Children's Sabbath, we give thanks for the precious gift of life and for all the children in the world
who represent our hope and our future.
We have brought them into a "What's next?" kind of
world: full of the harsh realities of nuclear weapons
and guns, snipers and terrorist cells, anthrax and
smallpox.
A world in which too many children can never hope for a
decent life.
A world where too many will not live long at all.
A world whose resources are tragically misdirected.

And so, today, O God, we pray for grace and for
transformation.
We understand that You can do no more *for* us than You
can do *through* us.

If we want to be blessed with health, then we must
participate in nurturing the well-being of our
bodies.

If we want a healthy world, then we must nurture the
well-being of our environment and the healing
of our broken connections to each other.

If we pray for peace, then we must become
more peaceful, turning away from war and
confrontation.

If we pray for love and reconciliation, then we cannot
hold anger and revenge in our hearts.

If we pray for understanding, we must not allow
dogma to get in the way.

If we pray for justice, we cannot allow unconscionable inequality in our own country.

And if we pray for our children, we must not tolerate
*in*tolerable conditions in the world we bequeath
to them.

O God, bless us, and teach us how to bless each other.

Bless us with the courage to overcome our wounds
and our wars and our hatreds.

Bless us with the faith that You are here in the persis-
tent power of goodness to overcome evil.

Help us to see Your face in the face of every child,
born into privilege or poverty.

Help us to choose a life that holds hope for all our
children, safeguarding a world that is for them,
as well as for us.

Amen.

The Language of God

Eternal and Loving God, who comes to us in the tumultuous noise of this world and in the silence of this sanctuary,

Teach us to pay attention to Your voice, for You speak to our hearts and to our hopes, if we would only stop and listen.

You speak to us in many languages . . .

> In the language of music and ritual and worship.
> In the language of confession and self-knowledge.
> In the language of forgiveness.
> In the language of creativity.
> In the language of conscience and justice.

Most of all, O God, You speak in the language of compassion.

> You speak through our deepest sense of connection to each other.
> You speak through the smallest acts of kindness.
> You speak through the courage to challenge all the forces of injustice and ignorance and prejudice that we allow to divide us.
> You speak through the poor.

> You speak through all who dare to place common
>   interest above self-interest.
> You speak through persons of all colors and back-
>   grounds and faiths who acknowledge that we
>   are made in one image, which is Yours.
> You speak through the universal hunger for justice,
>   the shared need for freedom and hope.
> You speak through our freedom to choose life over
>   death, reconciliation over vengeance.
> You speak through all who would nurture peace and
>   dialogue in a terrorized and warring world.

Teach us, O God, to listen. In the silence of this sanctuary
and the wisdom of our hearts, teach us to listen. We pray
today for our city and for our newly elected leaders. Help
us to find the courage and resources to rebuild this city
into a place of hope for all of its citizens, wealthy and poor.
Help us to claim a vision of justice that includes all of us.

Embrace us all with hope and with courage. Help us to
follow Your pathway to a world that can sustain us all.
In Christ's name we pray.
Amen.

Out of the Wilderness

God of Enduring and Steadfast Love,

Today we gather to renew our strength in Your presence.
We come to this place of worship like refugees from the
parched places of a wilderness we have created:

> A wilderness of human failure.
> A wilderness of escalating terrorism and hatreds.
> A wilderness of tragic and misguided war.
> A wilderness of leadership and vision.
> A wilderness of dysfunction—where the most power-
> ful nation on earth fails to provide decent health
> care or education, housing or emergency help to
> millions of its own citizens.
> A wilderness of greed and discrimination.
> A wilderness of broken promises and shredded safety
> nets.
> A wilderness of growing inequality.
> A wilderness of despair and fear and paralysis.

And so today, O God, we turn to You to nurture our
parched land, our parched world, our parched souls with
the living waters of Your love.

You once sent Your Son to remind us that You love us
all. To lead us out of the wilderness. To suffer with us. To
show us what it means to be created in Your image. He

came as Teacher and as Healer. He blessed the poor and
challenged the wealthy. He showed us how to be forgiving
and generous and inclusive. He brought courage to the
frightened, comfort to the grieving, hope to the poor and
the oppressed.

And so today, O God, we turn to You once again, and we
place our trust in You.

> May Your love and Your forgiveness flow like healing
> water into all the parched nooks and crannies of
> our hearts and minds and souls.
> May we begin to develop new root systems of con-
> nection and compassion and responsibility,
> nurtured by Your divine love.
> May we blossom into trees that bear fruit in the des-
> erts of human neglect and indifference.
> May our roots seek out the stream of Your love,
> growing deep, to sustain us through times of
> anxiety and drought.
> Help us all to join roots and hands and hearts in the
> repair of this world You have entrusted to our
> care.

O God, surround us all with Your love, Your mercy, Your
transforming, healing presence.
Amen.

Racism

Eternal God, who calls us to dismantle all the barriers and take down all the walls,

Gather us in today with Your extravagant, unfailing love. You are the God who sees *all* of us: young and old, abled and disabled, citizens and illegal immigrants, well paid and unemployed, born of different colors and creeds and sexual orientations, as made in Your divine image.

We come before You with all of our flaws, our conflicts, our longings and dreams. Help us to remember that Your divine seed, however deeply buried, lives within each one of us. And we must nurture it into life.

We pray today for healing, and for all who suffer injustice in our tragically divided nation and world. Help us to confront the shameful legacy of entrenched racism, entrenched privilege and power, entrenched poverty and prejudice: this festering wound that damages all of us.

Help us, O God, to become "the ones we have been waiting for." We know in our hearts that You do not intend for any of us to be imprisoned in roles of victim and victimizer. You do not intend for any of us to languish in impoverished human conditions of injustice or exploitation. Your love for all of us demands equal access to education, health care, opportunity, and hope. Help *us* to demand it also.

You are the God who sweeps aside all barriers; who declares that we are all Your children. You show no partiality. You are the one our *hearts* are waiting for. Guide us with courage and with generosity that we might acknowledge what is sacred in each one of us.

Help us to move toward the beloved community You intend—remembering, always, that Jesus came for all of us, loved all of us, suffered for all of us, died on a cross for all of us, that we might *all* be transformed.

We pray for humility. For the vision and moral clarity that will lead us to the healing so badly needed in our nation and in our world. O God, hold us, remold us, with the power of Your infinite love.
Amen.

God, Not Guns

O God, in whose eyes all are sacred,

We gather this morning to be reminded that we all belong to You. We confess that too often, we abandon each other. We come from a city and a country where unprecedented affluence overshadows invisible poverty. We tolerate too many forms of violence, discrimination, and racism. Violent inequality. Violent families. Violent streets. Violent neglect.

One of us dies by gunshot every eighteen minutes: thirty thousand of us every year! Even six-year-olds have been found with guns. Too many safety nets have been shredded. Too many of our children abandoned by an education system that fails them. Too many unarmed people of color shot by police. Too many men and women wasting away in overcrowded prisons. Too many courts meting out unequal justice. Too many unemployed and homeless. And we tolerate all this. But You do not!

And so we turn to You, O God, to recondition our hearts. Help us to relinquish violence in all its forms. Help us to embrace, not to fear, our differences. Help us to understand that what we do to others, we do to ourselves.

> If we hate others, we become hateful.
> If we withhold, we become withholding.

   If we judge, we become judgmental.
   If we fail to see each other's needs, we become blind.
   If we are forgiving, we find forgiveness.
   If we are compassionate, we become more loving.

Help us to build connections that cut across all the lines of religious and racial and cultural differences. To learn from those who may challenge our unexamined beliefs and assumptions.

Help us, as we worship today, to accept Your love, in which we are all made whole. Help us to build common ground: person to person, race to race, nation to nation, stranger to stranger. Help us to claim each other as brothers and sisters by treating each other with respect and dignity and openness. Teach us to be fair and inclusive. Help us all to understand that violence can never be stopped with violence. It can only be stopped with love.

Help us to see that our willingness to help each other is what makes us human. And our capacity to love is what makes us whole.

In Jesus' name we pray.
Amen.

Reverence

God of all Creation,

We gather to praise and worship You. You are the God who created all of us out of the same sacred clay. You formed us in Your womb, out of all the beautiful, multi-hued colors of our humanity, gay and straight, male and female. You made us each uniquely different, with a spark of Your divine nature in every one of us. Your breath in our lungs. Your love in each of our hearts. Your fingerprint on each of our souls. How magnificent the infinite beauty of Your creation: this world that includes all of us.

We confess today that we have allowed deep fault lines of prejudice and fear to wound and diminish us. Help us, O God, to address what is broken in our lives that we might reclaim what is whole, and therefore sacred.

Teach us to be reverent. For reverence will help us transcend all that we allow to separate us. Reverence is the forgotten voice in our many religions. In our struggle with diversity, it is reverence that establishes common ground. Without reverence, we will never become the fully human beings You created us to be. Without reverence, we will never reclaim what is sacred: our compassion, our capacity to love, our commitment to justice, our ability to honor one another as children of one God who loves us all.

Help us to remember today that Jesus *embodied* reverence.
He came for all of us. The privileged. The poor. The blind
and the lame. The immigrants. The mentally ill. The homeless. The adulterers. The heterosexuals and the homosexu-
als. The insiders and the outsiders of all our different
faiths and ethnicities. Jesus came to free us all! He came
for every child. Every man and woman. He came for the
cyclone victims of Myanmar. For the grieving parents and
lost children of southwest China. For the refugees of Palestine. For the starving of Somalia and Darfur, and many
other countries. For all who have fallen into the fault lines
of fundamentalist and ethnic violence. For all the victims
of intolerance and oppression and war that we create in
this divided world.

He came for every one of us at Riverside. Black, White,
Latino, Asian: for all the beautiful souls of this diverse
congregation! He came to awaken in all of us a sense of
what is possible.

O God, we pray for gratitude. For forgiveness. For healing.
And for Your love, which is big enough for all of us.

Help us to embrace all that is sacred in Your world.
Amen.

Blindness

Eternal God, who comes this day and every day into our midst,

We know that Your presence is everywhere around us, if we could only see. Whenever we permit You to enter our lives, our world is enlarged; and when we shut You out, our world is smaller.

In this hour of worship, we acknowledge the many ways in which we live in self-imposed darkness, blind to the light You offer as our God and as our guide. We live in isolation, treating each other as objects. We are blinded by fear, separated by prejudice and ignorance. We are blinded by self-interest. We are blinded by narrow assumptions that exclude the new and the contradictory. We are blind to the Son You sent as a healer, teaching us to *see* our neighbors as ourselves.

Teach us, O God, to see rightly—to see with our hearts. Teach us that we cannot and must not live for ourselves alone. Teach us that healing comes from the joining of human hearts, just as sin comes from separation. Teach us that we are made whole only when we see how fractured we are.

Today we acknowledge our need for a miracle, especially when confronted with our deep resistance to change. Help us to receive the gift of insight. Help us to accept Your love, which sees goodness in all of us, even when we feel lost in the darkness of sin. Help us to allow the power of Your love to shine in us, penetrating our darkness, lighting the way. Help us in this nation to overcome our blindness to the legitimate needs of the poor. To reclaim our vision: our generosity, our willingness to share our resources, our power, our intelligence. Help us to see that we will be whole only when no one is excluded from wholeness.

We ask this day that You empower with vision all who long for transformation and are prepared to join in the work of healing this troubled world. Resurrect in us the goodness and hope which can enter the world through every one of us. We pray to be held, all of us, in the transforming power of Your love.
Amen.

Church Conflict

G od of Grace and Mercy,

You are the creator of our world and of all that has life and hope and promise. Enter into each one of us this morning with Your sustaining love. In our troubled world, nation, church, how easily we forget that You are always beside us and behind us and within us.

> Capable of understanding, we often distort the truth.
> Capable of humility, we are arrogant and self-serving.
> Capable of facing hard truths, we cling to denial.
> Capable of insight, we are blinded by
>   self-righteousness.
> Capable of forgiveness, we resort to blame.
> Capable of inclusivity, we hide in the isolation of the
>   like-minded.
> Capable of learning from our history, we repeat our
>   errors over and over again.

And so, O God, we come to You today with our wounds, our brokenness, our conflicts, our longing. Help us to be still, in this noisy, turbulent world. Help us to listen for Your voice deep within us. Help us to believe that even in the darkest times, there is an ember of your divine light within each of us, which we must cradle and nurture into life. Empower us to become more like You. To reclaim our humanity and our goodness and our dignity. To be transformed by Your Spirit.

As we Riversiders face the difficult task of restructuring our church, of living with fewer resources, with the loss of people we love, people who lead, people who give, we ask that You empower us to make wise decisions. To move toward a common good. To learn the lessons that are necessary for our survival: the lessons of humility, generosity, compassion, peacemaking, justice, forgiveness, and love.

If Riverside is to be Your church—a sane voice in an increasingly insane country and world, then we must start with ourselves. Help us to deescalate anger and blame when there is conflict, that we might not dismember our own body. Teach us how to speak whatever truth is in our hearts with love, to acknowledge our fears and our flaws with greater humility, to explore differences with greater respect and dignity. To be clearheaded and compassionate. To become one holy family, each member committed to the other's welfare. Help us to follow the way of Jesus, who taught us to love each other as You have loved us.

We ask this day that You empower all of us to participate in the healing of our troubled church, our divided nation, our warring world. Teach us, O God, to love courageously. To overcome fear with faith. To seek the truth amidst contradictions. To remain open to hope. To be wholeheartedly grateful for all that sustains us. To make love our aim and faithfulness our pathway.

Today, O God, all of us need to be held in the power of Your divine love. Hold our beloved Dr. Forbes, and all the clergy, staff, lay leaders, and members who contribute to the life of this church. Sustain us all with Your vision and Your unfailing love.
Amen.

Touch

OLoving God,

Come to us as we gather today in worship. Gather us into Your holy arms, for we come needing Your touch. We come before You with all of our flaws, needing to be accepted. We come needing to be reminded that we are all made in Your image. That a tenacious seed of goodness lies dormant within us, waiting to be called forth by Your touch. And You do touch us!

You touch us with compassion when we fail You,
    with comfort when we suffer,
    with healing when we are broken.
Your touch holds us with love when we grieve.
Your touch softens our self-hatred with forgiveness.
Your touch inspires us to grow into the people we
    were created to become.

You bless the poor with Your touch.
You challenge the powerful.
You teach us that every single human being matters
    to You.
You ask us to be inclusive and generous.
You call us out of isolation.
Your touch opens our eyes to suffering and injustice.
Your touch empowers us to hold each other.

O God, touch us again and again, for we forget so easily.
Touch us with Your transforming power. Empower us,
now and always, to believe in You, that we might learn to
believe in ourselves. Touch us with Your sustaining love,
through which all things become possible.

In Christ's name we pray.
Amen.

Gay Pride Sunday

O God, who blesses us with the precious gift of life in all of its rich diversity,

Today we hear You calling us to be one inclusive family in which there is neither Jew nor Greek, slave nor free, male nor female. Today we acknowledge our need for Your love, which alone can dissolve all the fears that separate us. You have created us, in all of our diversity, to live in freedom. Yet we remain in bondage.

On this day when we celebrate gay pride—the pride we *all* need to have in ourselves whether we are black or white, gay or straight, privileged or poor—, the image of Matthew Shepherd hanging on a Wyoming fence still burns in our hearts and minds. We confess that too many dividing walls remain within us and between us:

> Walls of judgment,
> Walls of prejudice and fear,
> Walls of homophobia and racism,
> Walls of self-righteousness,
> Walls of dogma,
> Walls of ignorance.

Help us, O God, to take down the walls that blind us to each other and to You. Help us to deepen our awareness and our compassion, that we might see each other as people who share the same basic needs. Help us to *honor* Your diverse creation, not merely to tolerate it. Help us to respect the integrity of deep and loving connections wherever they occur: in blended families and divorced families and single-parent families, in homosexual as well as heterosexual unions and marriages. Help us to see that a human relationship must be judged by its inner worth rather than its outer appearance.

Help us to understand that we do not choose our skin color or our sexual orientation. But we *can* choose to be just and humble and loving. We *can* choose to address human suffering. We *can* choose to deliver life-saving drugs to dying nations and poor communities. We *can* choose to make decent health care a basic human right. We *can* choose to remember that the twelve million children orphaned by AIDS in Africa are our orphans too.

Today, as the gay and lesbian community celebrates pride in its identity, help all of us to learn to love ourselves and accept Your love for us, exactly as we are. Remind us that each and every one of us is made in Your image. Help us to overcome all that separates us from each other. For separation is the root of all violence. Help us to explore our differences and learn from each other. For we will never love the people we refuse to see or know. Teach us that we share too many flaws to stand in judgment of each other, and too many strengths not to be faithful to Your love for all of us. Help us rededicate ourselves to building a church, a city, a nation, a world where every person is valued as a child of God, and no one is excluded from the dignity and opportunity which each deserves.

Gay Pride Sunday

> Let us remember today that love bears all things,
> believes all things,
> endures all things!

In Jesus' name we pray.
Amen.

Gratitude

L oving God, who waits for us,

We come to You this morning with gratitude in our hearts.
As we gather now in the sanctuary we call home, we give
thanks for this congregation and for this church.

For the rich diversity that makes us whole—men and
women, gay and straight, people of every color,
young and old, privileged and struggling—we give
You thanks.
For echoes of truth and glimpses of faith.
For risks taken and wrongs forgiven.
For all who touch our hearts and nourish our souls, we
give You thanks.
For all among us in whom we sense Your presence.
For sustaining us with such extravagant love.
For the grace that enters our lives when we least expect it.
For hovering near us in the darkest moments of our lives.
For waiting for us when we have utterly lost You, we give
You thanks.
For the sanctuary we have all received.
For the music and the sheer beauty of this church.
For the chance to mend the broken fragments of our lives,
we give You thanks.

O God, help us as we worship to accept Your call to
transformation.

Help us to acknowledge our weaknesses, that we
might claim our strengths.

Help us to live in such a way that we harm no one,
and exclude no one.

Help us to share our resources.

Help us to participate in the stewardship of this precious world.

Teach us to be generous.

Work through us to do together the things we could
never accomplish on our own.

Help us to accept more fully and trust more deeply
the power that Christ revealed:

The power of truth,
The power of justice,
The power of forgiveness,
The power of compassion,
The power of unfailing love.

We ask, O God, that You hold us in the power of *this* love.
Hold the sick and the grieving, the isolated and the home-
less, the most powerful and the most powerless.
In Christ's name we pray.
Amen.

Becoming Gardeners

G od of Life,

We come seeking Your blessing. Today, as we honor our children, we remember that You are Father and Mother to all that is good in us. You know us before we are formed in the womb. You give birth to us. You consecrate us. You send us out into the world. You sustain us in our journeys.

Long ago, O God, You blessed us with a garden. You said, "Here is a garden filled with every living creature and plant. Care for it. Tend it. Remember the limits."

We confess, O God, that we have abandoned all the limits.

> We have polluted our garden and endangered our environment.
> We have filled it with weapons of mass destruction.
> We have allowed the rich to plunder it and the poor to starve in it, even while there is enough food for all.
> We have allowed diseases, which we can eradicate easily, to take the lives of millions.
> We have turned our backs on genocide and closed our eyes to injustices we could prevent.
> We have squandered the resources that sustain our lives.
> We have failed to tend and preserve Your garden for our children and for their children!

And yet, O God, You keep believing in us. And every child born is a blessing that contains seeds of hope that the world can be different. Help us to remember today that there is deep within each of our souls a seed which is created in Your image. That we must become gardeners of the soul to call this seed into life. That we must nurture the divine seed in all of us, before it can unfurl, reaching for the light of hope and love and connection.

Today, as we honor our precious children, help us to nurture the divine seed of every child, born into scarcity or abundance. Help us to be wise parents and leaders. Help our church and our world to provide leadership that we are proud of. For our children learn far more from living examples than from empty words. Help us to remember that we cannot pray for our children without acting to save them. No child should be homeless or hungry or sent into the world without education and health care. No child should be abandoned in a jail cell when abandonment got him there in the first place!

Help us, O God, to ensure that *this* church and *our* children are led by wise and compassionate leaders who can help us discern Your will and follow Your vision for our true potential at Riverside. Help us all to be faithful gardeners of the soil You have entrusted to our care. Amen.

The Good Shepherd

God our Shepherd and our Strength,

In our worship today, help us to open our hearts to Your steadfast love. In these times of high anxiety and deepening concern, we turn to You and to this sanctuary because we need to follow Your voice, Your guidance.

You are the faithful shepherd who always seeks out the lost and the strayed.

> You are the shepherd who promises that none of us
> will be excluded from the flock.
> Who watches over all of us, regardless of status or
> color, creed, or sexual orientation.
> You are the shepherd who promises to feed the strong
> and the weak with justice.
> But instead of heeding Your voice, we follow thieves
> and robbers who would lead us astray.

We confess that we have strayed far from Your safety. We live now in fields where the scale of human tragedy is growing every day. We have let in the thieves of limitless greed and widespread injustice. We have trusted robbers who pour billions into perpetual wars, sacrificing the legitimate needs of the most vulnerable among us. We have tolerated an overwhelming imbalance in wealth and resources that cripples the rest of the flock. We ignore the deep hunger for dignity and freedom and opportunity that human beings share all over the world.

Help us, O God, to learn to recognize Your voice, that we might follow You to safety.

> You teach us that we *are* what we *love*.
> That our only hope lies in the pathway of loving You and loving each other.
> That love requires us to respect each other, to acknowledge our common needs, to empower the weak, and to gather in the lost.
> To build a world energized by hope and accountability and vital connection.

Today we pray for all who are risking their own lives for dignity and freedom and hope. People cry out for help in many parts of our world. We pray for the many voices that are being silenced and betrayed by their own governments. We pray for wisdom and courage to bridge differences, to sow understanding where there is alienation, education where there is ignorance, hope where there is now only despair.

We pray now for all who are facing devastating floods, for all who are suffering in the catastrophic aftermath of natural disasters. We pray for our own flock here at Riverside who are in need of Your care and ours. Hold all of these in Your heart, O God, and help us to keep the faith, here in our own Riverside community. Help us to embrace and to build a new future together! To be forgiving and tolerant. To see each other, in all our diversity, all of our strengths and flaws, as loved by You. To eat and drink from the abundance of Your love for us.
Amen.

Domestic Violence

Merciful God,

We give thanks this morning for Your presence in our lives. You call us out of brokenness. Sometimes it is only Your love that holds us together; for we live by mending, and Your love is the glue. You come as healer, placing before us life and death, calling us to choose life. You comfort us. You guide us. You challenge us to become more whole. You forgive us. You stand by us when we are most lost and wounded.

Help us to understand that the healing of brokenness is not just an individual journey but a communal one that transcends nation and color and creed. You call us to become one spirit and body, honoring all the intricate parts that make us whole. How easily we forget that the whole body suffers when any part is in pain. That it is lethal to ignore pain in any part of our human body and community.

O God, we confess that too often we close our eyes to suffering. And we turn away from brothers and sisters who need our help. This includes the shameful silence in our churches and communities about domestic violence and abuse—that terrible darkness that invades the sacred sanctuary of families: betraying trust, shattering the very relationships depended upon for safety and protection.

Where there is darkness, O God, help us to light a candle. For only light will expose the truth that can set us free. Violence and sexual abuse in families violates every boundary of the victims: their bodies and psyches, their hearts and souls. When a family member betrays and violates a partner; a spouse; or an innocent, vulnerable child, the damage is real and lasting and sometimes deadly. And it must be stopped!

O God, we pray that all who are victims of violence and abuse might find the courage to speak the truth, to name the brutality, to seek safety and protection. We pray for their offenders to seek help in understanding the terrible damage of their actions. Help all of us, in churches and communities of faith, to shed the light of truth on this terrible darkness in people's lives.

Help us to understand that our capacity to help each other is what makes us human; that our capacity to love is what makes us whole. That hope and survival and dignity all depend on connection and compassion.

We are humbled by the abundance of Your love, O God, even when we fail each other miserably. Give us the grace to accept this love, through which redemption is always possible. Help us to understand that the human soul may be attacked, but is never destroyed because You are with us, holding our broken parts together with the power of Your love.

Today, we pray for all in our world who experience the violence of war, the violence of cruelty, the violence of poverty and powerlessness. We pray for women whose noses and ears are cut off for trying to leave their homes or their husbands. We pray for all the world's women and children who are powerless to protect themselves. We pray for peace in Afghanistan, in the Middle East, and in all parts of a world torn by conflict.

O God of mercy, hold all of us in the power of Your healing, mending love.
Amen.

What Love Requires

L oving God,

Once again, we gather to renew our strength in Yours. It is Your love that surrounds us in times of crisis and uncertainty. You are our ever-present help in times of danger. And when we stumble, it is Your light that shows us a pathway out of the darkness.

Today, O God, we have much to account for:

A country of deepening divisions,
A culture of selfishness,
A landscape of corporate bloat and spiritual
    starvation,
Unprecedented concentrations of wealth and greed,
A narrowing of opportunity,
A rescue plan that may never reach those most in
    need,
A world in which the powerful hijack the resources
    You intend for all of us.

Help us to remember that You are the gentle and powerful love that sustains us! Beyond all things. Within all things. You are all that we seek. All that we dream of. All that we come from. All that we might become.

Help us to remember that You sent Jesus as a message of Your love for us. We confess that we often forget this message—this powerful, compassionate, rule-breaking, inclusive, healing, and forgiving love that Jesus lived and taught. And when we forget, we are diminished. How easily we forget that You have called us to a pathway embraced by *every* faith: to love one another even as You love us.

Help us today to live in the bigness, the radical inclusivity of Your love. It is a love that requires us to acknowledge each other's yearnings, each other's humanity all over the world. This world we share is full of broken promises, poverty, warring ideologies and faiths, nuclear threats, starvation and disease. Your love calls us to a new Kingdom where we participate in saving each other because we are all worth saving.

Your love requires us to have bigger hearts:

> Imaginative hearts that will invent a way to beat swords into plowshares.
> Honest hearts that will recognize evil and confront injustice.
> Humble hearts that acknowledge our failings.
> Wise hearts that will take responsibility.
> Forgiving hearts that can let go of blame and revenge.
> Generous hearts that respond to suffering with compassion.

This is the love that Jesus brought to our lives. Help us to believe in it, to follow it, to be transformed by it. For in this love, all things are possible.
Amen.

Called to Communion

Eternal God, Mother and Father of us all—of every person and nation, every color and faith,

This morning we give thanks for Your unfailing presence in our lives. On this day, we come to Your table to break bread together. Help us to remember that You created us as one body. It is the body You formed from dust long ago:

> Your hands molding us, shaping us.
> Your breath breathing life into our lungs.
> Your love assuring us that we are all created in Your image—a divine spark of Your light in each of us.

Today we acknowledge that the communion You call us to is hard to find. That covenants with You and with each other are widely broken. All over the world, we see evidence that the foundational stones of faith are used too often for throwing, too seldom for building. We see the broken covenants of our nation, bent on blaming the poor and protecting the wealthy. The broken covenants to protect the environment and the future You have entrusted to our care. We confess that we all struggle with diversity. Afraid of the unknown. Afraid of our future together.

O God, may the many signs of struggle and suffering in this time serve to point us in the right direction. Teach us that the foundation of any faith must be built on compassion, not dogma. Teach us that mutual respect is Your most fundamental law.

Today we mourn the tragic suicide of Tyler Clementi, a young student whose privacy was violated in the most abusive and public way possible. This horrific betrayal calls out to us to respect the dignity of every human being! This is the most fundamental requirement of our faith—as Christians, Muslims, Jews, Hindus, Buddhists, Humanists. It is not negotiable. It is a matter of life and death!

So before we come to Your table today to share the gift of bread and cup—Christ's body, sacrificed to save all of us; Christ's blood, calling us all into covenant with You—, let us come clean. Cleansed of all that divides us—our prejudices, our resentments, our fears, our pettiness, our betrayals, our rigidities. Before we come to Your table, let us remember that Christ crossed every boundary of separation, broke down every barrier between us. Let us remember that love is the only requirement for communion. And as Your servants, we must follow the commandment to love, or we shall surely perish.

We pray today for all the peoples of the world. We pray for all who continue to suffer in the hardship of natural disasters, of brutal wars, and of terrible poverty. We pray for Your abiding love.
Amen.

Called to a Beloved Community

God of the Living Waters,

Help us to pray today with our hearts, for our words have no power without our hearts. In this wilderness of sin, we are sustained by Your limitless and empowering love for all of us. You call us to wholeness even when we are at our most broken. You do not fail us or lose us, even when we are lost and so clearly failing each other. You call us into Your circle of love.

O God, we confess today that we need You. We live in a world of deepening poverty. Of entrenched hatreds and fears. Of escalating conflicts over scarce resources. We live in a time when dictatorships are toppling and democracies unraveling. A world that has become steadily more materialistic and spiritually impoverished. Ruled increasingly by the powerful, for the powerful. We are witnessing the unraveling of the economy and the jobs that sustain it. The unraveling of safety nets that have helped to protect the poor and the elderly. The unraveling of opportunity for the young, of access to decent education and housing and health care for larger and larger parts of our human family. We turn blind eyes to the unfair burdens carried by African Americans and Hispanics. We will not finally revoke a death penalty that is brutal and wrong, that kills too many who are innocent and is administered with deeply racist injustice.

Help us to see, O God, that You cannot change this world for us. You can only change it *through* us. The seeds of healing, the seeds of transformation and peace, are within each one of us. But there will be no healing in this world until we make room for it in our hearts, by clearing out our hatreds and fears and our tragic dehumanization of each other.

This week, fourteen-year-old Jamey Rodemeyer, a vulnerable gay child—Your child—our child, took his own life. A victim of bullying and humiliation and intolerance. We are all responsible for his death! Help us to understand the prophet's cry: where there is no vision, no compassion, the people will perish. Without vision there is no hope. And hope is the most precious of all our human resources. We simply cannot live without it. And we have been pushing our children, our country, our world, right to the brink.

We pray today, O God, to be led by Your vision of a beloved community. Challenged and renewed by Your love for every one of us. It was with love that You created us in Your image, capable of free will. *Fundamental* to our humanity is this capacity You gave us all—to choose good over evil, generosity over greed, compassion over indifference. It is Your radically inclusive love that allows us to see that our lives are deeply intertwined. That we cannot sustain a world where self-will runs riot, and the powerful exploit the weak.

O God, You are the heart big enough for all of us.

> You are love.
> You are challenge.
> You are forgiveness.
> You are hope.
> You are life.

Help us right here, in our beloved Riverside, to make more room for each other with all of our differences. Help us to be loving and forgiving. To be proud of our aspirations and humbled by our failure to live up to them. Help us to be held and guided by Christ's incomparable spirit and courage. Bless us with faith that in the journey ahead, You are with us and within us.

Bring to us all the promise that new life—resurrection—is possible in our floundering world.

O God, we place our trust in You. Grant us wisdom and courage and love for the living of these days.
Amen.

Three

Seasons of Longing

"Free Our Hearts to Faith and Praise"

> *"The soul that rises with us, our life's star,*
> *Hath had elsewhere its setting,*
> *and cometh from afar . . ."*
>
> —WILLIAM WORDSWORTH,
> *ODE ON INTIMATIONS OF IMMORTALITY*

Invocation

OLoving God,

Here we are again, trying to follow You on this journey. Evangelists, seekers, doubters, some strong in faith, some faltering, some feeling whole, and others fractured . . . we are a magnificent, conflicted, contentious, hopeful community of very diverse folk, who all carry some seed of You in our hearts. Help that seed to take root and grow into Your intended fullness. Help us to abandon the arrogant assumption that we can become anything worthy without You.

Humble us that we might walk with You, listen to You, learn from You. Help us to unearth the gifts You have placed in each of us. Help us to trust that still, small voice that reminds us that You love each and every one of us, faults and all. Teach us to be Your servants, holding the gift of this, Your world and Your church, in reverence and humility.
Amen.

Martin Luther King Sunday

God of Peace,

We come to You this morning searching for the hidden wellspring, the oasis, that makes the desert beautiful.

Today we remember the life of a man, Martin Luther King, who had revolutionary vision because he was guided by a great love, a dream worth fighting for, and the courage to speak the truth.

Today, O God, we pray for love, for truth, and for courage. We confess once again the sinful gap between what You call us to be and what we are. We confess that we are still more comfortable with blame than with responsibility. That we see the injuries we have suffered but not the injuries we have caused, especially those that stem from unacknowledged racism. We confess that our nation squanders precious resources on the largest, most powerful military in human history. That we persist in policies that abandon and blame the poor, erode our civil liberties, undermine equal opportunity for minorities, and sabotage honest dialogue. That we refuse to renounce the violence of war, the entrenched injustice of our economic policies, the deep corruption of institutionalized racism.

We worship the golden calves of self-righteousness and materialism and power. We ignore the sacred virtues of humility, compassion, and justice.

O God, help us to find the courage in this wounded world
to live in the largeness and generosity of Your heart. For
Your heart, Your love, nurtures the seed of goodness that
lies dormant in every person, race, religion, and culture.

> Your love requires us to include all our brothers and
> sisters.
> Your love asks us to stop demonizing "the other." To
> see the log in our own eyes. To be humble and
> self-scrutinizing.
> Your love sees that when one of us is diminished, we
> are *all* diminished.
> Your love binds us as one people.
> Your love challenges us to uproot the still sweeping
> racism that saps our country's humanity.
> Your love teaches us to find each other if we would
> find You, and to love each other if we would
> love You.

Grant us, O God, the courage to seek peaceful solutions to
the entrenched hatreds that divide our international community of "haves" and "have-nots." Grant us the wisdom
to make the world safer not with military power but with
a peace based on mercy and justice. Grant us greater understanding of the mutual needs that bind us all together.
Help us all to bridge differences, to welcome dialogue, to
listen with our hearts.

Help us *all* to bring good news to the poor; to proclaim
release to the captives; to let the oppressed go free, so that
justice and reconciliation will prevail for all the people of
our land.

In Jesus' name we pray.
Amen.

Homecoming

God of Love and Hope,

As we gather this morning under the joyful banners of our ministries and programs, we give thanks for this sanctuary we call home.

> We come from places far and near, some of us restored, some hurting.
> We come because You sustain us with Your love, day in and day out.
> We come from a world of violence and suffering.
> We come to be strengthened and nourished.
> We come for Your acceptance, Your guidance, Your forgiveness.
> We come to be transformed by Your love, which promises that we are all worth saving, and that we must participate in saving each other.
> We come because You remind us of what our nation too often forgets: that the whole human community is deeply connected.

Today, O God, we remember the life-changing, world-shattering tragedy of 9/11. As we pray for all who died that day, and for all the heroic men and women who tried to help them, we pray also for the many other peoples of the world who are victims of extremism and bigotry, racism and violence.

We confess now that we live in the shadow of 9/11. It is
a shadow that reaches around the world. A shadow that
has spawned two tragic and ill-begotten wars, tens of
thousands of deaths, and unimaginable suffering. It is the
shadow of intolerance and fear and bigotry. Too many in
our country color all Muslims as radical Islamists. It is a
shadow over the American dream:

> A dream of inclusivity and diversity and mutual
> respect.
> A dream of religious tolerance.
> A dream that says that Ground Zero belongs to all
> of us—Protestants, Catholics, Jews, Muslims,
> Atheists, Hindus, Buddhists, Humanists—, who
> come from every walk of life to build a nation
> where we can live in peace and mutual respect,
> with liberty, justice, and opportunity for all.
> It is a dream betrayed by many of our elected
> politicians and undermined by fanaticism and
> bigotry.

We confess, O God, that we have fallen far from Your path.
You teach us that there are many colors and creeds in Your
Kingdom, but only one heart. It is the heart of love and
compassion, justice and forgiveness, and You placed its
promise in all of us. Help us to remember that when we
demonize and dehumanize each other, we diminish ourselves, and we endanger the whole fragile world we share
in common.

O God, the seeds of evil and the seeds of Your goodness
and love exist in all of us. Help us to be conscious, responsible cultivators of the better seeds of our nature, and to

confront the worst. In our relationships. In our church. In our nation. In this world that belongs to all of us!

We pray today for all who live in the shadow of fear and intolerance. We pray for all who try to be peacemakers in the Middle East, and in many other troubled parts of the world. We pray for the misguided Florida pastor who tragically believes that burning Korans could ever be God's will or Christ's intention. We pray that we might all remember Your most basic teaching: to love our neighbors as ourselves.

Lord, make us instruments of Your peace.
Amen.

World Communion Sunday

God of Hope,

It is Your amazing grace that sustains us through darkness and light, in all the seasons of our lives. On this day of World Communion, our powder-keg world is threatened by poverty and ignorance, injustice and unfulfilled dreams. We are very fragile. And so we come before You to break bread together; for strength, for hope, and to remember You.

We need to remember that You created us to be one global family, diverse in culture, color, and creed, but united in the deeply human needs that we have in common. We need to remember Your fundamental injunction: to love You we must love each other. You are the God who taught us all to make sacrifices not for You, but for each other. It is enough, You said, "to do justice, to love mercy, to walk humbly with our God." Are we even trying?

In creation, O God, You endowed us with the freedom to choose whether or not to follow You. We confess that our recent choices have been disastrous. Our eyes are blinded by arrogance. Our government is filled with self-righteousness. Our leaders are intoxicated with power. Help us to remember that our capacity to choose is what makes us human. But choosing a path of love and compassion is the only option that can make us whole.

We can choose to renounce violence.

We can share our technologies, our food, our
medicines.

We can preserve the environment for all of our
children.

We can refuse to tolerate intolerable conditions of
suffering in a world that belongs to all of us.

And we can admit that prosperity built on the suffering of others will lead only to moral bankruptcy.

O God, help us all to be wiser: to see that we are all Your
children, and that You are asking all of us—Christians,
Muslims, Jews, Palestinians, Israelis, every race and nation—to respect each other. Be merciful to us all, for we
have all sinned. Help us to pursue peace, not power.

Help us O God, to remember that nothing can separate us
from the power of Your love.
Amen.

Advent

God of Blessing,

Today, in this season of darkness, as we watch and wait for a child of hope to enter our anxious world, help us to remember that it is always darkest before the dawn.

O God, open our hearts to Your love, our eyes to Your light, our ears to Your call. For You come, in this darkness, to search for us.

> You come as mystery, arriving in the humble, the hidden, the unexpected.
> You come in the midst of war and natural disaster, AIDS and cholera, calling us to live with courage and with love.
> You come for the jobless, the homeless, and the hungry, calling us to empower the poor and the forgotten.
> You come to challenge the cowardly moral indifference that is corrupting our corridors of privilege and power.
> You come for the marginalized, for the immigrants, for the multitudes of men and women and children who are denied any room at the inn.
> You come to teach us that war will never be a pathway to lasting peace.

You come as the Father who sees that we have made a
great mess of Your Kingdom.
You come as the Mother who nurtures us to a fuller
humanity.
You come as faith that sustains us through loss and
disappointment, danger and despair.
You come for the faithful and the lost!
You come for all of us.

O God, bless today this offering of gifts for the children of
incarcerated mothers and fathers. Help us to acknowledge
that all the children of the world must become sacred and
precious to *us*, as they are to You. For so many of them
need to find safety in a peaceful manger and hope in a Star
that illumines a darkened sky.

In this season of waiting, O God, help us all to see that it
is *You* who is waiting for *us*. May Your Spirit awaken our
capacity for justice and compassion. May the many signs
of suffering—all the Bethlehems of our time—, guide us
toward a world that can only be made safer with justice
and goodwill.

We pray for peace within and peace without, in our unwise
nation and in our bungled, bloodied world. We pray today
for North Korea, for China, for Iran, for Afghanistan, Iraq
and Pakistan, and for the United States in its complicated
role in the Middle East and in the larger world. May all of
our leaders find courage and wisdom to guide us through
these treacherous times.

Help us to be steadfast in our love and courageous in our
faith.
Amen.

Christmas Eve

God of Hope,

On this holy night we give thanks for all the love You poured into us through that child born in an unlikely manger. Born then, as now, into a world littered with indifference and violence and poverty. Born to bring an extravagant love into an impoverished world.

> A love that casts out fear.
> A love that is perfect and forgiving and redeeming.
> A love that holds us close throughout our lives.

May this love be born in our hearts that we might release our own goodness and hope into the world.

On this holy night, may new life be poured into us, reminding us that every child is holy and deserves room at the inn.

> May we, like Mary, find the courage to give birth to hope.
> May we, like Joseph, accept the difficult challenges of faith.
> May we, like shepherds, seek out all who are lost.
> May we, like Magi, search long and hard for wisdom.

In this dark night, may we find a star to light the pathways toward peace and healing in our fractured world. And may this child called Jesus, born anew in our hearts, awaken us to all that is possible in these impossible times.

O Come, O Come Emmanuel. God is with us.
Amen.

Lent: You Are There

Eternally Compassionate God,
Guide us in this season of Lent as we try to follow Jesus
through the wilderness. As we travel into uncertainty,
through our own temptations and hidden inner regions,
keep us close to You.

> Keep us on course when we stumble into self-decep-
> tion and self-righteousness.
> Keep us from being quick to judge and slow to
> forgive.
> Keep us from demonizing others and failing to con-
> front our own complicity in sin.
> Keep us from yielding to the temptations of arro-
> gance and power.
> Keep us from the plague of materialism that blinds us
> to the needs of others.
> Lead us all back to You. Show us the way to healing
> and reconciliation and peace in our struggling
> world.

O God, help us to learn how to search for You in the wilderness. For we will find You in our hearts.

> Whenever we acknowledge that we are all Your chil-
> dren, You are there.
> Whenever Your love for us empowers us to love one
> another, You are there.

Whenever the darkness of ignorance and prejudice
is replaced by the light of understanding and
solidarity, You are there.

Whenever we recognize something sacred, something of You in every human being You have
created, You are there.

Whenever we understand that human brutality takes
root in the soil of human desperation, You are
there.

Whenever we challenge despair and cynicism with
the promise that You have the power to make
all things new, and Your love transforms us, You
are there.

Whenever we act with generosity and compassion,
seeking peace and justice in a world created for
all of us, You are there.

Whenever we remember that the heart of our humanity is kindness, You are there!

Today as we look toward the cross, we remember the many
corners of our world where suffering is a daily reality and
resurrection a distant dream. We pray today for the people
of Lebanon and all the tenuous movements toward democracy and peace in the Middle East. We pray for all the
civilians and military so deeply affected by the violence of
war. We pray for the victims of genocide in Sudan, and for
the multitudes in Africa and many other countries who die
in needless poverty every day. We pray for all our brothers
and sisters who are in prisons, and for those far and wide
whose paths are unimaginably difficult.

O God, we pray for healing and strength for all we have
named, and for all who are named only in our hearts. May
we open our minds and souls to receive the love You are
always ready to give. Amen.

Palm Sunday

God of Compassion and Love,

In this holy week, we come to You to guide us through our unholy world.

> Today we hold high the palms of hopes and
> expectations.
> Today we gather in the jubilant crowd of all who
> want to follow Jesus to Jerusalem.
> Today we are reminded of all the times when You
> give us hope and courage.

With the gift of Jesus You entered into our lives to show us the path You want us to follow.

> On this path we find not a triumphant king, but a
> humble servant who is willing to walk with us
> and suffer with us.
> On this path we find a crown of painful thorns and a
> torturous cross.
> We see that Jesus walks with humility and obedience,
> each step requiring courage and commitment.
> We see flash before our eyes a life dedicated to peace
> and healing, a love that excluded no one, an
> unprecedented inclusivity that reached out to
> all who were deemed unclean and impure and
> unacceptable.

We see a wisdom that transformed people's lives, a vision of justice that challenged and threatened the powerful. A light strong enough to penetrate the darkness of human sin. If we follow, we know that this light, this pathway of Jesus, will lead us to new life—to resurrection. His pathway leads to compassion and to love.

O God, help us, on this Palm Sunday, to trust You.

You enter this Good Friday world of ours, so filled with violence and intolerance and injustice, and You say, "Trust me—follow me to a new Kingdom." And we see how difficult it is.

You are asking us to abandon violence.

You are asking us to look into the human abyss of neglect and indifference, of terrorism and nuclear proliferation, of abusive power and greed.

You are asking us to overcome ethnic and religious intolerance, and to live as members of one holy family. To question all the ways in which we benefit from privilege and injustice.

You are asking us to be brothers and sisters—regardless of color, creed, or sexual orientation.

You are asking all of us: Christians, Muslims, Jews, Israelis, Americans, Palestinians, Africans, black and white and every color of the human rainbow, to make peace! To find ways to sustain life for all of us. To be forgiving and connected, generous and compassionate.

O God, help us to follow Your path.

Help us to trust that You walk with us every day and will never abandon us. Help us to trust that new life—resurrection—is possible through You, and that nothing can separate us from the power of Your love for each and every one of us.

O God, surround us with this love.

For in the power of Your love, we are afflicted but not crushed, persecuted but not forsaken, struck down but never destroyed.

In Christ's name we pray.
Amen.

Easter Invocation

Spirit of the Living God,

Fall afresh on us. Meet us, mold us, fill us, use us.[1] O God,
You call us out of the shadow of a Good Friday world—full
of betrayal and suffering. You call us into the mystery of
Easter—the promise that Your love and Spirit, embodied
in the life of Jesus, could not be snuffed out by his death.

Grant us now the grace and the courage to live in Your
world—our world—with Christ's love alive in us. Freeing
us from sin, calling us to new life and new ways of living
together in freedom.

Teach us that we are not so small or so flawed that You
cannot work through each and every one of us. May our
doubts be overcome. May the miracle of resurrection give
us courage to give birth to new life: helping us to transform our brokenness and claim our full humanity.

Sustain us with Your love, through which all things are
possible—even miracles.

Spirit of the living God, fall afresh on us.

Amen.

---

1. From Daniel Iverson's (1935) hymn, "Spirit of the Living God,"
published by Moody Press.

Pentecost

S pirit of Fire,

On this day of Pentecost, we gather once again in this sacred space, and we pray for Your Holy Spirit to come upon us.

Today we humbly confess our need for transformation.
We confess our need for Your Spirit in our world, which is so fragmented, so lost, so driven by self-interest and communal neglect.
We confess that we have failed to love our neighbors as ourselves.

> That we insist on our own way.
> That we are neither patient nor kind.
> That we rely more on power than on faith.
> That we protect the rich and neglect the poor.
> That we resist Your Spirit and Your teaching.
> That we utterly fail to love one another as You love all of us.

Help us, O God, to listen to Your many tongues. Teach us to listen with our hearts.

> You speak to us in all of our diverse languages and cultures and perspectives.
> You speak in the universal language of compassion and empathy.

You speak in the language of peace and
reconciliation.
You speak in the language of reflection and insight.
You speak in the language of human needs and
rights.
You speak in every cry for justice.
You speak in the language of generosity and
accountability.
You speak in the language of hope.

When we listen to this voice, we are transformed. And we
know that You hold us all in Your hands.[2]

"You hold you and me, brother, in Your hands.
You hold you and me, sister, in Your hands.
You hold the little bitty baby in Your hands.
You hold black and white together, gay and straight
together, rich and poor together, in Your hands.
You hold Riverside together in Your hands.
You hold the whole world in Your hands."

Hold us today, as we gather in this diverse community.
Guide us with the power of Your vision for what we might
become with faith in You.

Teach us, through the power of the Holy Spirit, to
serve You by living with greater courage and
compassion.
Teach us to worship together, and live together, with
greater humility and greater love.
Teach us to become aware of the unnecessary ways
in which we hurt each other and perpetuate

2. From the traditional African American Spiritual "He's Got the
Whole World in His Hands."

injustice or indifference. Show us what it means
to become human beings who are guided by
that tiny spark of the divine that lives in each
one of us.
Teach us to make love our aim, for love bears all
things, believes all things, endures all things.

We pray today for healing in the lives of all among us who
are ill or grieving or fighting lonely battles with despair.
We pray for all the innocent victims of terror and war,
natural disaster, or human indifference in our troubled
world. We pray for a spirit of unity and love to guide all of
our world's leaders. We pray for sanity and for peace.

O God, help us all to become agents of healing and hope
in our world.

In Jesus' name we pray.
Amen.

All Saints Day

Eternal God, in whose eyes all are sacred,

Enter into our hearts this day that we might be sustained
and guided by the power of Your presence in our lives.
Today we come with gratitude for all who have finished
the race, and while running it helped to shape the soul
of our congregation here at Riverside. We give thanks
for Harry Emerson Fosdick, for Martin Luther King, for
William Sloane Coffin, and for all the prophetic voices
that have left their imprints on our hearts. We give thanks
for all the loved ones—mothers, fathers, family members,
friends—who have departed over the past year. Help us to
internalize and keep alive all that they taught us, that we
might fulfill our own potential and promise here on earth.

Death calls us to treasure the precious gift of life.

> Help us, O God, to see that every life is sacred.
> Help us to break the bonds of fear and prejudice that
> separate us one from another. For life depends
> on connection.
> Help us to acknowledge our ignorance. For life de-
> pends on knowledge.
> Help us to open ourselves to each other. For life de-
> pends on openness.
> Help us to have compassion for one another. For life
> depends on compassion.

> Help us to respect all our brothers and sisters. For life
> depends on respect.
> Help us to embrace our differences. For life depends
> on diversity.
> Help us to love generously and courageously. For life
> depends on love.
> Help us to remember that nothing—not even death—
> can separate us from Your enduring love. We
> come from You. We return to You when we die.

We give thanks for Your faithfulness every step along the
way.
Amen.

Sending Forth Dr. Forbes

A Benediction

O God, our Strength and our Foundation,

We ask that You hold out Your hand to all of us at Riverside, that we might walk in Your presence into our future.

We gather to celebrate and say goodbye to this deeply
loved, irreplaceable man who has touched our lives
and hearts and shaped our faith for nearly two decades.
Preacher and Prophet. Pastor and Poet. Generous. Magi-
cal. Loving. Jim Forbes has brought such a powerful light
into our world. For it is Your light that shines in him and
through him. Even when he was discouraged, he always
brought us Your light.

It is the light that sees all of us—young and old, black and
white, gay and straight, privileged and poor—as made in
Your image. It is the light that steadies us when we stumble. That helps us find common ground in our diversity.
That shines in the darkest night of our souls and shows us
the potential that lies dormant in every flawed one of us.

It is the light we need in this country, diminished by arrogance, by the abuse of power, by the abandonment of the most powerless among us. It is the light we need to forge new pathways of healing in our divided world. A light that makes us bigger than our smallness. And stronger than our weakness.

We give thanks, O God, for all the light that Jim Forbes has brought to us. As we send him forth, help us to trust the love You have for all of us and for him. Be with him as he carries a much-needed voice of truth and prophetic justice to the larger world. Be with us as a church, finding our way. May Your Spirit guide us. Your forgiveness humble us. Your love empower us. Grant us wisdom and grant us courage for the living of these days.

And to our beloved Pastor, we say:

> Go forth with our love.
> Go forth with our gratitude.
> Go forth with courage and faith.
> Take your light to the world,
> And let it Shine; let it Shine; let it Shine!

Let the whole church say,
Amen.